ANITA MATHIAS

THE STORY OF DIRK WILLEMS:
The Man who Died to Save His Enemy

BENEDICTION CLASSICS

ISBN: 978-1-78943-044-8
© 2019 Benediction Classics, Oxford.

The Story of Dirk Willems:
The Man who Died to Save His Enemy

The banging shook the old timber-framed house in Asperen, Holland.

"Open in the name of the Duke of Alva," rough voices yelled. The horses clopped on the cobbled street, their breath rising in impatient clouds.

A slight young man ran down and unbolted the door.

"Are you the Anabaptist Dirk Willems?" the Burgomaster demanded. The mail-clad soldiers surrounding him glared.

"I am."

"Do you admit that in 1521 at the age of twenty, contrary to the doctrines of the One Holy Catholic and Apostolic Church, you were re-baptised in Rotterdam, at the house of one Pieter Willems?"

"I was indeed baptised as an adult after I made a public profession of my faith in the Lord Jesus. For according to the example of the Lord, that is the right and proper time to be baptised."

"Never mind that. Have you taught that Christians should not bear arms, nor take oaths of loyalty to The Most Noble Duke of Alva?"

"I have indeed taught that. For, in the Sermon on the Mount, the Lord commanded us not to resist evil, nor to take oaths. Mindful of the invisible presence of Christ, our word, spoken to another human being, should suffice."

"Never mind all that. Have you unlawfully permitted people to be baptised in your house?"

"I have."

"Will you renounce all your heretical beliefs, teachings, and actions?"

"I will not, for I have resolved to obey the commands of the Lord Jesus as closely as I can. For…"

"Never mind all that. Thief-catcher, in the name of the Duke of Alva, arrest this man," the Burgomaster commanded.

* * *

During the Reformation, Christianity stretched, and shook herself awake, rubbing sleep from her eyes. It was a Renaissance of the Spirit. Ordinary men and women rediscovered Scripture, reading it for the first time—not in Latin but in their mother tongues—reading hungrily, as if it were news, breaking news, good news.

Martin Luther, then an Augustinian monk, desperately sought spiritual perfection by means of spiritual disciplines, including fasts, which permanently ruined his digestion. *If ever a monk got to heaven by his monkery, it was I. If I had kept on any longer, I should have killed myself with vigils, prayers, and readings,* he wrote.

Hoping to distract him from his tormenting guilt, his Superior, Dr. Johann von Staupitz, promoted him to Professor of Biblical Studies at the University of Wittenberg. Luther immersed himself in the Bible while lecturing through it, and was dazzled by its language. He truly believed that he was dealing with the very words of God. *God is in every syllable. No iota is in vain,* he wrote.

As he understood the Book of Romans for the first time—that God accepts us as his beloved children, not because of our good deeds, but because of our faith in Jesus—Luther declared, *"Thereupon I felt myself to be reborn and to have gone through open doors into paradise."*

When Martin Luther visited Rome as a pilgrim in 1510, he was appalled by the worldliness, extravagance and cynicism, particularly in the aggressive selling of "indulgences" spearheaded by Johann Tetzel. Buying indulgences promised Catholics a shorter period of suffering, purging, in Purgatory after death; the money was used to fund the building of St. Peter's Basilica, as well as the exquisite art of Michelangelo, Bramante, Bernini, and Raphael.

Luther was appalled at Tetzel's saying, "As soon as a coin in the coffer rings, a soul from purgatory springs." *Who knows if it is really true?* he wondered about this papally-sanctioned doctrine. And with that question, he began, one by one, to question every Catholic doctrine that lacked any Biblical foundation, or was expressly forbidden by Scripture.

In 1517, Luther pinned Ninety-five Theses on a church door in Wittenberg, challenging Catholic practices—the sale of Indulgences, Confession, Purgatory—that he considered unscriptural.

The Ninety-five Theses were wild fire. Within two weeks, they created an uproar throughout Germany; within two months, thanks to Gutenberg's printing press, they were read and discussed all over Europe.

In Switzerland, the influential reformer Huldrych Zwingli went further than Luther, only accepting those doctrines and practices that had a firm Biblical foundation, and ignoring every Catholic doctrine without it-- such as a celibate priesthood, the veneration of saints, the Pope's power to excommunicate, the damnation of the unbaptised, hellfire and, especially, tithing.

* * *

At the same time, however, there were wilder, dreamier men and women, dubbed the "Radical Reformation." They dreamed not only of a private, internal reformation, but of communities in which each member obeyed the voice of the Spirit within them, obeyed the indwelling Christ, and obeyed scripture.

They publicly confessed their faith in Christ, repented of their sin, and amended their lives. And *then* they were baptised. Again. And so, they were scornfully called "Anabaptists," or "re-baptisers"—a label they rejected since they believed that infant baptism, not being a conscious choice, was no baptism at all. However, the mocking monicker stuck.

The Anabaptists believed that the Holy Spirit still spoke directly, and that God still gave some men and women the gift of prophecy. They were egalitarian, treating both men and women, rich and poor, as equals in their close-knit communities, modelled on those in the Book of Acts. They practised simplicity—in their food, dress and speech. They were honest, gentle and peaceable; even their harshest critics said so.

Their faith set them ablaze. They resolved to obey the Sermon on the Mount, their "Bible within the Bible," as precisely as possible. To experience the blessings promised in the Beatitudes to those who choose the way of meekness, mercy, and peace-making. To refuse to quarrel and contend. To love their enemies and pray for their persecutors.

They believed in pacifism, oh yes!—in turning the other cheek, and letting the aggressor seize both coat and cloak. They believed Christians should never bear arms, despite the threat to Reformed communities from the Turks in Austria and Germany, and the Catholic armies in Reformed Northern Europe.

Their Schleithem Confession read: *"Therefore there will also unquestionably fall from us the unchristian, devilish weapons of force—such as sword and armour, and all their use either for friends or against enemies—by virtue of the Word of Christ: Resist not him that is evil."*

* * *

They were persecuted--of course, they were. By Catholics; by Lutherans; by Zwinglians, all of whom were offended by the Anabaptists' desire to re-baptise the baptised. The Anabaptist desire to create communities of "true Christians" within Christian cities like Zurich provoked outrage. Also, since refusing to bear arms or to take oaths to rulers or magistrates meant self-exclusion from civil or military service, the Anabaptists threatened the established order!

Anabaptism was made a crime, punishable by death, in European country after country. Some Anabaptists were flayed and had their tongues torn out. Others were drowned with deliberate and ironic cruelty, after the Holy Roman Emperor Ferdinand I sardonically called drowning "the third baptism, and the best antidote to Anabaptism." Many Anabaptists were beheaded, tortured to death, or drawn and quartered. Still more were burned at the stake.

* * *

When Dirk Willems was arrested in Holland in 1569, he refused to recant the radical reading of Scripture which had set his life ablaze with purpose and joy. The Crown confiscated all his property for its own uses, and he was sentenced to be "executed with fire, until death ensues." Willems was imprisoned at the Palace in Asperen, until May, when he was to be publicly burnt at the stake.

Autumn passed, and it was winter. Looking out of the prison window one December night, Dirk Willems noticed that the moat around the castle had frozen solid.

His heart beat faster. Had the Lord provided a means of escape? Might the Lord Jesus enable him too to walk on water?

Willems ripped his bedsheet, knotted the rags together, tied one end to the window and slowly climbed down, the cloth supporting his body, grown skeletal on meagre rations in the long months of imprisonment.

He tiptoed onto the ice. And it bore his weight.

The stars shone bright in the frosty night. He skidded across the pond, remembering the nights of his youth, skating with his friends who loved the Lord Jesus on the frozen ponds of Rotterdam. He felt as if he were flying.

The Lord Jesus was rescuing him from his enemies.

* * *

"Stop! I command you in the name of the Duke of Alva: Stop!" he heard the palace guard shout, but using his last reserves of strength, Dirk slid across the ice of the moat, the Hondegat.

Behind him the guard, "the thief-catcher," raced across the ice, handcuffs in hand, closing in, closing in.

"Lord Jesus, I ask in your name! Help me. Please," Dirk prayed as he slid across the ice.

And now he scrambled onto solid ground. He kissed the icy earth.

Delivered by Jesus.

* * *

"Willems, help me! Help me, please."

Dirk turned round. The ice across which he, grown emaciated in captivity, had slid, lithe as a cat, had cracked beneath the weight of the burly thief-catcher. He could no longer see the guard's body, just his thrashing hands, one of them gripping handcuffs. As the man grabbed at the ice, it shattered into a myriad pieces.

The guard was drowning.

As Dirk paused beneath the starry skies, the words of the Lord Jesus, which he had recited to himself, again and again, through hungry days and sleepless nights returned like distant music.

Love your enemies, do good to those who hate you; bless those who curse you; pray for those who persecute you.

Do not resist evil.

And Paul's words: *Do not be overcome by evil, but overcome evil with good.*

"Dirk Willems, help me. Help!" the guard gasped, clutching the ice which splintered as he grabbed it, only his head now visible, and his hand, his hand with the shackles.

Under the silent stars, Dirk halted. Prayed. And then, "I will do it for the love of the Lord Jesus," he decided in a rush of resolution.

For the love of the Lord Jesus whom he had resolved to obey in all things; for whose sake he had chosen imprisonment rather than pretend to accept Catholic doctrines he did not believe; for the love of Jesus whom he had decided to follow, whether it led to happiness or death, Dirk Willems turned around.

He glided on the ice as far as he dared, and extended his hand to his enemy, the guard. And pulled him to safety.

They stood on solid ice. His voice quavering with cold and emotion, the guard said, "Thank you, Dirk Willems.

* * *

But the Burgomaster, who stood watching outside the Palace walls, called out across the moat, "Remember the oaths you swore to the Duke of Alva, thief-catcher. You swore to catch criminals and deliver them to justice. I command you in the name of the Duke of Alva, seize the heretic."

The thief-catcher hesitated. Then muttering, "Forgive me," he grabbed Willems's wrist, clapped the handcuffs on him, and dragged him across the drawbridge, back to the castle.

Willems was now confined to a small, barred room at the top of a tall church tower, his feet cramped in wooden leg stocks. He was tortured. He did not renounce his faith.

On 16 May 1569, he was led out to be burned to death outside Asperen.

* * *

It was a blustery day. A strong east wind blew the flames away from his chest, after they burnt the flesh on his lower body. His suffering was long and lingering. Willem's loud cries were heard in the town of Leerdam, towards which the wind blew.

"O my Lord, my God," he called out, over seventy times.

Finally, unable to watch his torment, the supervising judge wheeled his horse around and commanded the executioner, "Dispatch the man with a quick death."

* * *

Sometimes we walk through a dark forest by the light of a star which had died ten thousand years ago.

Dirk Willems, fool for Christ, you are one of the "children of God without fault who shine like stars in the sky." Your light still blazes five hundred years later.

We, who are amazed at your goodness, salute you.

We are astonished by your love for Scripture: you did not compromise your understanding of it, even though that meant imprisonment and the loss of your property, your freedom, your health, and your life. We are stunned by your integrity.

But, most of all, we are moved by how you helped your enemy, though it meant your certain death

We are inspired by how you kept your eyes on the Lord Jesus through the long agony of that barbaric burning.

We believe that, as you died, heaven opened, and you saw Christ standing at the right hand of the Father, ready to welcome you.

And we know you are with him, shining, in the great golden cloud of witnesses, the communion of saints which sweetens the earth.

Dirk Willems, this world was not worthy of you. You did not get to write your story, but you lived a beautiful one.

Thank you.

About the Author

Anita Mathias is the author of *Wandering Between Two Worlds* (Benediction Classics, 2007) and a children's book, *Francesco, Artist of Florence: The Man Who Gave Too Much*. She has won a writing fellowship from The National Endowment for the Arts, and her writing has appeared in *The Washington Post*, *The London Magazine*, *Commonweal*, *America*, *The Christian Century*, and *The Best Spiritual Writing* anthologies. She has blogged for Tearfund in Cambodia.

Anita has a BA and MA in English from Somerville College, Oxford University, and an MA in Creative Writing from the Ohio State University. She lives in Oxford, England with her husband and daughters, and blogs at anitamathias.com.

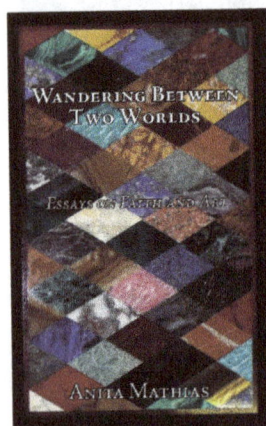

Wandering Between Two Worlds: Essays on Faith and Art
Anita Mathias
Benediction Books, 2007
152 pages
ISBN: 0955373700

In these wide-ranging lyrical essays, Anita Mathias writes, in lush, lovely prose, of her naughty Catholic childhood in Jamshedpur, India; her large, eccentric family in Mangalore, a sea-coast town converted by the Portuguese in the sixteenth century; her rebellion and atheism as a teenager in her Himalayan boarding school, run by German missionary nuns, St. Mary's Convent, Nainital; and her abrupt religious conversion after which she entered Mother Teresa's convent in Calcutta as a novice. Later rich, elegant essays explore the dualities of her life as a writer, mother, and Christian in the United States-- Domesticity and Art, Writing and Prayer, and the experience of being "an alien and stranger" as an immigrant in America, sensing the need for roots.

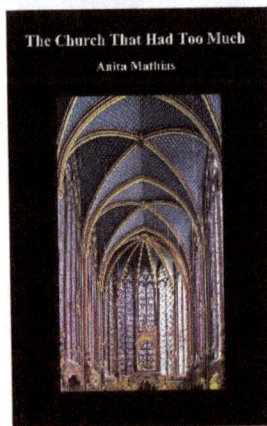

The Church That Had Too Much
Anita Mathias
Benediction Books, 2010
52 pages
ISBN: 9781849026567

The Church That Had Too Much was very well-intentioned. She wanted to love God, she wanted to love people, but she was both hampered by her muchness and the abundance of her possessions, and beset by ambition, power struggles and snobbery. Read about the surprising way The Church That Had Too Much began to resolve her problems in this deceptively simple and enchanting fable.

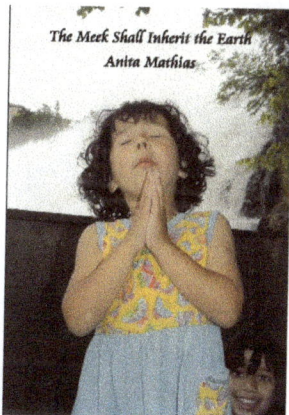

The Meek Shall Inherit The Earth
Anita Mathias
Benediction Books, 2013
38 pages
ISBN: 9781781393956

"Blessed are the meek, for they shall inherit the earth," Jesus says in his most puzzling Beatitude. Puzzling, because, if we are honest, it does not feel true to our experience. So do the meek inherit the earth? Is this true? Or isn't it? In *The Meek Shall Inherit the Earth*, an extended meditation on the power of gentleness, Anita Mathias grapples with this mystifying Beatitude.

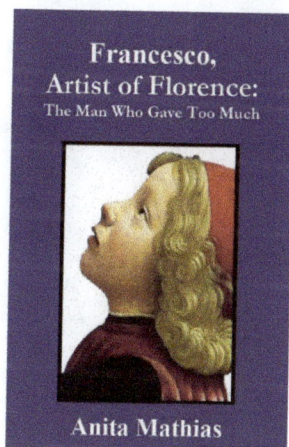

Francesco, Artist of Florence: The Man Who Gave Too Much
Anita Mathias
Benediction Books, 2014
52 pages (full colour)
ISBN: 978-1781394175

In this lavishly illustrated book by Anita Mathias, Francesco, artist of Florence, creates magic in pietre dure, inlaying precious stones in marble in life-like "paintings." While he works, placing lapis lazuli birds on clocks, and jade dragonflies on vases, he is purely happy. However, he must sell his art to support his family. Francesco, who is incorrigibly soft-hearted, cannot stand up to his haggling customers. He ends up almost giving away an exquisite jewellery box to Signora Farnese's bambina, who stands, captivated, gazing at a jade parrot nibbling a cherry. Signora Stallardi uses her daughter's wedding to cajole him into discounting his rainbowed marriage chest. His old friend Girolamo bullies him into letting him have the opulent table he hoped to sell to the Medici almost at cost. Carrara is raising the price of marble; the price of gems keeps rising. His wife is in despair. Francesco fears ruin.

* * *

Sitting in the church of Santa Maria Novella at Mass, very worried, Francesco hears the words of Christ. The lilies of the field and the birds of the air do not worry, yet their Heavenly Father looks after them. As He will look after us. He resolves not to worry. And as he repeats the prayer the Saviour taught us, Francesco resolves to forgive the friends and neighbours who repeatedly put their own interests above his. But can he forgive himself for his own weakness, as he waits for the eternal city of gold whose walls are made of jasper, whose gates are made of pearls, and whose foundations are sapphire, emerald, ruby and amethyst? There time and money shall be no more, the lion shall live with the lamb, and we shall dwell trustfully together. Francesco leaves Santa Maria Novella, resolving to trust the One who told him to live like the lilies and the birds, deciding to forgive those who haggled him into bad bargains--while making a little resolution for the future.

www.ingramcontent.com/pod-product-compliance
Lightning Source LLC
Chambersburg PA
CBHW080538030426
42337CB00023B/4791